How to Write a Novel

Ingredients to a Bestselling Book

Emma Fisher

i

CONTENTS

Introduction   v

1   The Land of Imagination   1

2   Mapping a Story   5

3   Character Creation   11

4   World Building   15

5   Drafts and Second Drafts   16

6   Selling Your Work   27

    Conclusion   33

INTRODUCTION

Storytelling is as old as civilization itself. Since we were first able to open our mouths and communicate, pick up a utensil and start writing or drawing, we've been telling stories to each other. It's part of the human experience. Stories serve as entertainment and as lessons. We use books to both fill the long hours of the day and to impart lessons about life. Today books haven't changed too much in their purpose.

We still read to entertain ourselves, to warn ourselves about the path we're on. Some books warn of the future, sometimes they reignite the past. Books are limitless and only defined by the edges of your imagination. Books have started wars (see: *Uncle Tom's Cabin*) and scared an entire generation (see: *1984*).

Perhaps you've had this idea brewing in your head for years and years. Maybe you've been planning it in notebooks, scribbling it in the corner of homework or reports for work or even on a park bench at your lunch hour. But the problem is…

Where do you begin? How does the first page become the last page and how does one sentence become thousands of them? It's an incredibly process if you think about it, building up word upon word until, suddenly, you have an entire story.

Books just don't appear out of thin air. You don't suddenly have a word document filled with 100k words. So how do you get from a blank page and an idea to the full book, filled with well-crafted prose, memorable characters, witty dialogue, and enough heart to get the attention and the emotions of the reader? It's not an easy process, and most of it is going to be on you, your own discipline and your own skills.

But that doesn't mean you can't ask for a place to start and some guidance along the way. So, cheers to you for finally deciding to pursue that book in your head. This guide is a way to help you start off your work. The rest will be up to you…

THANK YOU FOR BUYING THIS PINNACLE PUBLISHERS BOOK!

Join our mailing list and get updates on new releases, deals, bonus content and other great books from Pinnacle Publishers. We also give away a new eBook every week completely free!

Scan the Above QR Code to Sign Up

Or visit us online to sign up at
www.pinnaclepublish.com/newsletter

CHAPTER 1: THE LAND OF IMAGINATION

A writer (specifically Denis Johnson, author of *Jesus' Son*) once told me while in school that you should ignore those stories that live in your head for years, the ones you always promise yourself you're going to write because you will never get to them, there's a reason they've lived in your head for so long and not been set free on the pages of a book.

I don't agree with that. Though, at the time, young 20-something me thought I was being given some sacred knowledge. I thought to my own story that had been living in my head in many incarnations since I was 13 years old. I decided he was right, I was never going to get around to it and I should let it go. Today I'm well passed my college graduation, writing books professionally, and I still think about that story.

There's a reason for that.

Some stories are going to stick with you forever and there's nothing you can do about that. They're going to live in your head until you decide to do something with them. And, despite what other accomplished writers will tell you, there is a reason for that and you shouldn't ignore them. After all, how many authors out there tell stories about how their magnum opus works lived inside their head for years and years before they finally were able to get them down on paper and turn the story into what they imagined.

George RR Martin has been working on *A Song of Ice and Fire* since the 90s, Stephen King started the *Dark Tower* series in the 80s. These are the stories that lived in brains and matured over time. They needed room to breathe and germinate without contamination from outside forces. Keeping stories and ideas and characters locked up in your head for a while is part of writing, and it's not a bad part of it. It's where all great stories start, in the imagination pool inside your head.

You might have had this story brewing inside you since you were a teenager, or maybe you thought of it, like JK Rowling and the *Harry Potter* series, while on a train ride. A fleeting thought can turn into an entire world, but they're all going to need time to become something great. That's where you need to learn to allow for patience, matriculation, and the ever-inching forward wheel of time.

The fact of the matter is; stories need to live in your brain for a while. You need to toss them around like you might work down a hard candy in your mouth. How long do you think a sculpture stares at a brick of marble? Why is it any different for a writer? You need to stare at your giant block of marble too and get at the story underneath. And sometimes that's going to take a lot longer than you think. *Lord of the Rings* was planned and written in the course of a month. You need time for these things and that's okay.

One of the biggest flaws a writer will have is the curse of impatience. You're going to see the work in all its completeness and you're going to want to get to that point as quickly as possible. There's nothing wrong with that, eagerness and energy is needed, especially if you work full time when you're not writing. But you can't expect yourself to have a fully completed work in a few days or a few weeks or even a few months. Even if you can get a draft out, there are all sorts of editing that needs to happen.

So these things live in the land of imagination inside your head. That's fine. But that doesn't mean you shouldn't interact with them while they're there, waiting to be born. Sitting there and staring at the idea like a static painting won't help much, and there are ways to work with a story as you're coming up with it. The land of imagination is an ever moving, living place, after all.

Who is Involved?

Many writers have different approaches when it comes to starting a work. Some people start with genres, plots, general ideas. But the best way to start that's going to help you, in the long run, is figuring out who the characters are. These aren't going to be just names and physical descriptions. These are actual people, they're going to make up your world, make choices that push the plot forward. We'll get into more in-depth ways to go about character creation later in the book, but for now, you'll want to get yourself a rough idea of who the characters are, or at least who your main character is and why it matters.

What is the Genre?

This can be a tricky step. Genre is, at its core, a marketing term used to categorize and define a work to best sell it to a demographic. It's not something you should focus on too much because genre conventions can trip you up if you think about them too much while writing. That being said, you need to have an idea of what kind of story you're telling. Is it horror? Romance? A western? Fantasy? That's all you really need, just one word to go off of. Later you can let publishers and agents worry about hitting "target demographics" and "markets" and all that jargon that has no place in art.

What is the Setting?

This becomes particularly important in various subgenres of fantasy work. But it's important to understand the setting no matter where your book takes place. A mastery of the setting, of the descriptive factors that reveal it, is one of the best ways to get the reader to trust you as you were through writing your work. You can make the world feel incredibly real and incredibly visceral by knowing exactly where your characters are. For this, it often helps for writers to set works in places they live in and are familiar with (such as Stephen King's affinity for setting stories in New England).

You don't have to hold yourself to just setting stories in your hometown or the place where you went to school. But you need to know the place you're setting your story, especially if it's a real city because there are readers out there who do live there and will quickly call you on your bluffs if you've got too many. In that regard, sometimes setting a story in a real world setting can be a lot more dangerous.

With fantasy, you have the freedom to do whatever you want

where the setting is involved. And when it's a fantasy story, that means your setting isn't just a place where things happen, it's a place where an entire history has taken place. Fantasy settings (and any setting for that matter) means language and history and current events and politics. You can't simply say your story is set on the continent of Tauriel or on Bleecker Street in Chicago and not talk about who the rulers are, who the people living here also are, what the recent history is. The setting can be a character in and of itself (*The Hunchback of Notre Dame* is a famous example that casts Notre Dame as a character itself).

How Does It End?

This is crucial. Many writers out there will claim they like to write without knowing the ending, preferring to discover it along the way. There's nothing wrong with discovering a story as you go, figuring out the plot points and twists as they happen. But you need to have an end point in sight. You need to be moving towards something. It's not unlike being back in school: you were always headed for that June end date, you weren't sure exactly what was going to happen along the way, but you knew how it was going to end. Writing a book is no different. If you have no destination in mind, then your journey will be all over the place.

There are other things to consider as you move through it all. But most of it is going to be fully fleshed out in the following sections. Writing is both segmented and compartmentalized and an organic flow of several processes at once. The balance of that, knowing when to step back and when to blend it all together, is the part that's tricky and something you'll have to make your own. But if you follow these parts, focus on these elements, and give the writing your all, then you'll have yourself a novel you're proud of.

CHAPTER 2: MAPPING A STORY

There are several ways you could go about mapping your story. I refrain from calling it "outlining" since that feels a bit final and that terminology can be a bit of a buzzword to past papers you had to write in school and other fewer fun memories. This isn't an outline, it's not something you're going to be married to. This is mapping a story; it's setting up a path you can follow if you desire. You can change it.

Types of Writers

George RR Martin talks about two types of writers when it comes to the planning and writing phase of the work. Put simply: the gardener and the architect. It might surprise you to hear which one of these two types of writers Martin is and is probably indicative of his abilities to get his final two books complete.

- **The Gardener:** This type of writer is fairly hands off when it comes to dictating how the story is going to be going. This is the type of person now interested in excessive planning but planting seeds and watching them grow with a bit of help and control. It can be a scary way to go about writings for some people.

- **The Architect:** This writer is on the other end of the

spectrum. This person is someone who needs the story very much laid out in the most complete way possible. This can mean different things to different people but, ultimately, it means knowing a more detailed version of the events of your story enough to have a guide to follow if you needed it.

Personally, I find the best course of action is to aim for somewhere in the middle of these two ends of the spectrum. If you're enamored with a concept and don't feel the need to truly wait before you jump right into a world, that's okay, you can go for it. If you're nervous and want some structured support for the story you're trying to tell, that's okay too. But if you're just starting out, if this is your very first story then there are some ways you can help yourself with outlines and planning to make things less scary when the time comes to face that first, blank page.

Types of Outlines

There's a couple officially ways of doing this and then there are ways that I made up based on what I've done in the past and what works. You can feel free to employ any of these styles, any combination of them, or make your own. There's no wrong way to outline a story, but there are some that work better than others.

- The Hero's Journey: This is the mother of all story structures and one that's been found in virtually every story told since the dawn of intelligence. The Hero's Journey has its roots in the *Epic of Gilgamesh*, the world's first written story and one, you could argue, we're all simply rewriting. But it was defined in the 20th century by Joseph Campbell in his book *Hero with a Thousand Faces*, which became the basis for the original Star Wars trilogy. It follows this basic pattern:

  ○ The Call: the hero first hears the "call to adventure"

  ○ Refusal of the Call: the hero, because of current

circumstances or fears, refuses the possibility of adventure

O Supernatural Aid: after the hero commits to the quest, a sagely guide enters as a mentor

O The First Threshold: this is the first test and the moment the hero leaves their old world behind forever

O Belly of the Whale: the final separation from the old world into the new one

O Road of Trials: a series of tests (often in threes) that begin the transformation for the hero

O Meeting the Goddess: the moment where the hero experiences an all-encompassing love (can be romantic, platonic, or familial)

O Temptation: the hero is tempted to abandon the quest

O Atonement with the Father: the hero takes on that which has the most control over their life

O Apotheosis: the hero dies in some physical or metaphorical way and experiences an enlightenment as a result

O The Ultimate Boon: the hero achieves the goal of their quest

O Master of Two Worlds: the hero has achieved harmony in their inner worlds and in their exterior ones

O Freedom to Live: the hero is free to live a changed life with no regret

Now, there are some steps that I skipped because this is the general barebones outline. If you need something more in depth, there are versions of that out there (such as several steps during the return portion of the journey). This is a great way to outline any story, from a fantasy epic to a piece of literary fiction because every character goes through a hero's journey. That's the way we've designed stories since the beginning of time. But you don't have to use this one to guide your world you're creating.

- Dan Harmon's Story Circle: This is a version of the above monomyth that has been designed to be more character based. For someone hesitant to implement an outline that seems to be designed for fantasy epics, this might be the route you want to go for your story to get the effect without getting bogged down in details

O Zone of Comfort: the hero exists in their static world

O They Want Something: while existing in this world, they have a want that has not been met yet

O They Go to Get It: They make the decision to go after the thing they desire

O Adaptation: while on this quest to get what they want, they have to adapt to this new world they're in both emotionally and physically

O They Get What They Wanted: the hero finds and gets that thing they'd been looking for

○ Consequences: but there is a price to pay for the thing they desired

○ The Return: the hero returns to where their journey started

○ Change: they realize the change they've gone through and can move forward with more knowledge

As you can see, both options deal with personal change for a character, though Harmon's version takes out environmental factors in the character development: it's all coming from the desires within and the choices the hero has made to get the thing they want. It's an option for someone not too concerned with how the world will play against their character. While it may seem like the genre is going to have a lot to say about which one of these options you take, it's not that simple (consider Margaret Atwood's dystopian story *The Handmaid's Tale* which is considered a work of literary fiction by many).

- Traditional Arc: this version employs that triangle structure that we've all been taught since we were in grade school: current state, catalyst, rising action, climax, and falling action. There are certainly some more detailed versions of this out in the world and you can use them as well, but this basic story structure is a tried and true method. It's a great way to start, to get the barebones of how your story will go, but, in my opinion, you're going to want more detail on certain parts before you get to writing based on this structure

- Chapter by Chapter: this is a very involved method and one I wouldn't suggest undertaking until you've utilized one of the above methods in some way to get a sense for your characters and story. It's also not the best place to start if this is your first book. You should certainly have a chapter by chapter outline at some point before you start truly writing but don't make it the place you go to right off the bat or else you'll be setting yourself up for some frustration. That being said, once you're ready for it how you outline your chapters is really up to you and the story elements you want to be included.

So, I think we've covered several options you now have for mapping out a story and getting yourself into a position of getting the scaffolding of the story down before you start. It's important to know where you're going and what's going to happen, but few things are as important as knowing who your characters are and why they matter.

CHAPTER 3: CHARACTER CREATION

The first and most important thing to remember about a character is that they are a living, breathing person. You're not making a two-dimensional cut-out that exists to say lines and move the plot forward. These are real people and you're going to be sharing snippets of their lives with your readers. Think about it just in terms of yourself…how many memories to you have? How far back do they go? What was the first job you ever wanted? How many times have you changed what your favorite color is? What was the first toy you remember getting? Who was your first crush and second crush and third?

A lot of things make up a person. Syd Field had an excellent explanation for a character in his lectures of screenwriting: characteristics are a set of facts and qualities about someone, a character is a series of choices. What makes up the sum of your character is not nearly as important as the choices they're going to make. That being said, you do need an outline of the characteristics before you get started on giving them choice.

So, where's a good place to start for building characters? Well first, I imagine you have an idea of who some of these people are, even if it's something as simple as "hero, "villain", "mentor", etc. There's nothing wrong with thinking about characters in terms of the roles they will fill in the story but you want to make sure that they're more than that. They're people first, who happen to be doing this service to the story.

Names

Before you do anything else, you want to start with naming your characters. They need names. You can't refer to them as character's A, B, and C up until the moment you start writing. The first thing you learn about anyone is their name and your characters deserve the same courtesy. You'll want to get used to calling them by their names and knowing them that way. So this is an important and integral first step in the process.

There are many methods you could take to accomplish this portion of the writing process. Sometimes names just pop out and they stick, but sometimes you want a little more meaning behind them. You may have noted, in the past, that many characters have names that hint at their personality and their role in the story. One famous and very straight forward example is Darth Vader whose name translates to dark father in Dutch. In To Kill a Mockingbird, the man who was wrongly charged and convicted of rape was named Tom Robinson, the bird-centric last name eluding to the famous line about it being a "sin" to kill a mockingbird.

This is called an aptronym and happens in real life too, coincidently. William Wordsworth was a poet, Margaret Court was an Australian tennis player, Sara Blizzard is a BBC meteorologist, among others. While these real world examples are a bit on the nose, you can easily name your characters based on elements of their personality and roles they're going to play in the story. You can start by looking up names on baby naming websites and books to discern the meaning of names. This can also be an aid for factual and practical reasons since you can search by popular baby names in different eras and regions.

But once you've got a name, use it. Call this person who and what they are. Get used to it, make sure it sounds real and believable to you because, if it doesn't, it will have the same off-putting effect on your readers as well. But, once you've got a name, you've got the stepping stones of a great story ahead.

Character Sheets

During the character creation process, many people will turn to character sheets for guidance. You can find these all over the internet and many people like to utilize ones outlined for things like Dungeon and Dragons and other role-playing games. Some are more detailed than others, going into pages and pages of details while some fill out the logistical basics needed to make a functional person (job, pets, etc.) A combination of these two levels of detail is what's going to make the best sense in the long run for you. You know how much you need and don't need but it's always best to err on the side of too much over too little. The more you know about your character, the more secure you'll feel in writing about them and their world. While you may not need to know that their absolute favorite food is the pasta their mom makes at Christmas, it could help if you suddenly find yourself searching for what their favorite food might be in the middle of a scene.

You can't predict everything you're going to need. But the more prepared you are, the fuller and more real your character is going to seem to the audience, which can only ever be a good a thing. So any sort of little details you think about yourself (maybe a freckle you don't like, an inherited trait, your favorite comfort food) make a note of it for your character as well, throw in little ideas for them to feel more real and fuller.

Choices

After this, you're going to be doing a lot of your character building on the job. The most important part of your character is the choices they make and that can only really be hashed out by writing out the story and getting the plot out there. That doesn't mean go completely blind and just assume what will be will be. But it does mean you don't have to put the burden on yourself to know everything instantly.

That being said, there are some big plot points and choices you'll need to know. For example, if someone is going to betray a character, that's a vital part of their role and who they are so you'll want to know that. But little things will come as they come. That's gardening style author version of this that you'll want to utilize. But remember that while these choices may come as they come, they're the most important part of what makes a person tick in the world you create.

I NEED YOUR HELP

I really want to thank you again for reading this book. Hopefully you have liked it so far and have been receiving value from it. Lots of effort was put into making sure that it provides as much content as possible to you and that I cover as much as I can.

If you've found this book helpful, then I'd like to ask you a favor. Would you be kind enough to leave a review for it on Amazon? It would be greatly appreciated!

CHAPTER 4: WORLD BUILDING

Now, you may be saying to yourself "I'm writing literary fiction, I don't NEED to create a world" and you'd be correct but not as correct as you think. Here's the deal, every world needs building. Even if it's 2017 New York City you're still creating a fictional version of it to share with the world and that requires you to come up with some details and histories. These people you're creating aren't real, so you need to give them a past (think of it like in season 5 of *Buffy* when Dawn was inserted into everyone's lives and given an entire past and memories).

There are different levels of world building and there are different intricate details that you could be dealing with but you're still building a world where there was not one previously, putting people where they did not exist in our world, so you need to build that world. Maybe it's slight in the future and you have to imagine what the stock market will be like in fall 2017 or slightly in the past and you need to remember what life was like in summer 2012. You'd be surprised how important these details are to creating the world.

Level 1: The Real World

You could be writing a story about the old lady who lives a reclusive life at the end of Spooner Lane, reliving her history as she talks about going to protests for Vietnam and living through the AIDS crisis. It takes place on a real street in a suburb of Chicago, in the modern 2017 world. But that doesn't mean you don't have to construct a set of conditions for this place. Maybe there's construction going on, maybe everyone on the street moved away, maybe a group of college students moved in next door.

It's microcosmic, but it's important. You need to create a context for this little world we're going to be looking at. Is there a cat who wanders the neighborhood? Is there a kid who plays music from his car too loudly whenever he drives home from school?

This is starting to sound like a lot isn't it? We don't think how often the small details of life can affect our goings on. To help keep this organized and give you an idea of what details are important, I've put together a list of questions you can work off of to get yourself started based on a logical progression someone would take entertaining a house...

- Where are we? What's the house number? Is the doorbell working? Is there a creak on the front step? Does the door swing shut or do you have to pull it a bit?

- What's the smell when you first cross the threshold? Is there a decoration that catches your eye? Is it a two story house? Can you see the kitchen? The living room?

- Is the house clean? Does it smell like the last meal cooked there? What was the last meal? Is there music playing?

- Is there a backyard? Does it have a barbecue? Is it clean? Are there weeds? Is there a path worn into the grass from where people often walk?

Are you starting to get the idea? This is just one place to start for building the small world this story takes place in. You can apply these questions to virtually any part of the world (the street, the grocery store, the public transit, and on and on it goes). This is the easiest way to world build, these are the building blocks since these same questions need to be asked for any of the world building that you're doing.

Level 2: Real World...But Not Quite

This is one to use for historical fiction, futuristic settings, or doing alt-history work. For this, we're still going to use those same questions from above, as mentioned, but we're going to be throwing a slight spin on them. Because we need to figure out a larger history of this place and where it differs from the version of history we know now. So first things first, exactly how familiar is this place? Is it a version of history where the Nazis won? Is it the future where America is a monarchy again? Is it a fictional tale of a soldier during the Revolution? You should, of course, already know this, but if it's historical fiction, art history, or speculative future matters for how we're going to go about building this world.

So, the first thing you'll want to ask yourself is what is different about this world, what makes it something like our world but not quite? *The Hunger Games* is an example of a dystopian future where the states are gone and reorganized into districts based on the historic industry of the area they inhabit. This style of world calls on both the new (the creation of the government system of Panem) and the hold (historically the Appalachians have been coal miners, the Gulf of Mexico has been a huge fishing exporter, etc.). *Her* and *I, Robot* both imagine the progressing future of artificial intelligence, taking place in a slightly evolved version of our world. The idea of the futuristic approach is imagining the world as it is now and wondering how it will progress (or in some cases, regress) based on historical events and current affairs.

But maybe you want to know how things would be in a what if scenario? *Man in the High Castle* imagines a version of modern day America under the control of Nazi Germany who won World War II. What's different? What would be the same? What are defining characteristics? Would Apple have been developed? Hybrid cars? Would certain art forms have come to fruition? Maybe it's less bombastic than Hitler taking control of the US and more to do with smaller, personal changes (like the film *Anastasia* that imagines the grand duchess survived her family's execution). For any of these types of stories, you need to have a solid understanding of how the world works now and look at what's integral about what you're changing. This takes a bit of research, more than you might realize.

Level 3: Magical Realism

This is one step up from the two real world levels because these types of stories often imagine some kind of secret world or secret rules to the world beneath the real one. One example is *Bless Me Ultima*, a young adult novel telling the story of Antonio in the American southwest and the magic that has existed in the land for generations. This type of story is going to rely on a completely convincing view of the world but with a fair about of magic under the surface.

Another great example is *Bridge to Terabithia* that tells the story of a young man and his female friend who invent a fantasy world in the creek by her house. It blends the real world of middle school with a fairy world just outside the back porch, bringing them together effortlessly. Some worlds are more involved, such as *Wild Sheep Chase* that imagines an existential and cynical world of magical realism. There's also gothic versions of this level such as *Big Fish* that takes the tall tales of an old man, portraying them as he tells them (including Siamese side show twins, an actual giant, a haunted forest, a town trapped in the 19th century hiding in the woods and other embellishments on real events).

Arguably, this is the world that gives you the most freedom. You've got the real world but how much you want to make the magic part of it, how fantastical you want it, is all up to you and virtually limitless. It can be as crazy as you want or as calm. It can be as overt as you want or as subtle. The nice thing about magical realism is you don't really need to establish rules for this the way you do with other fantasy worlds. This one is one that readers will accept at face value without excessive explanation or the need to know the exact do's and don'ts so fit. So if you want a fantasy world without the layers of building and less need to be a rule follower, this is a great place for you to start. From here you could even branch into things like urban fantasy and other subgenres.

Level 4: Your Fantasy World

This is the big one and it comes in many forms and many faces. Ultimately, the way this breaks down is this: low and high fantasy. Either one of those worlds comes with its own levels. Simply put, high fantasy is your run of the mill *Lord of the Rings, Dungeons and Dragons, Game of Thrones* style of story. It's sometimes also called swords and sorcery fantasy. It takes place in another world where magic and mythical creatures and warriors are running rampant. Low fantasy is a form of fantasy that's another step up from urban fantasy and magical realism, it's stories like *Harry Potter, Percy Jackson,* and *His Dark Materials.*

Now, there are some discrepancies. *Tuck Everlasting* is sometimes billed as low fantasy and other times billed as magical realism. There's overlap and there's room to make arguments, but either way, the breakdown between low and high becomes pretty clear, regardless.

So let's start where things are easy and we've already covered a lot of it: low fantasy. Specifically, in terms of something like *Harry Potter,* this is a fantasy story that takes place in a world we can conceive of, one that's familiar, but has too much magic and otherworldly elements going on in it to be magical realism. There are dragons and sorcerers and duels and potions but it takes place in late 20th century England, making it grounded in the real world and, thus, not high fantasy. But you get the gist.

Building a world like this is often found in young adult works. Stories like this one, Percy Jackson, and *Artemis Fowl* all take place in the world we recognize but a version of it where magic is real. For this, you're still going to need to build up that world. After all, think how many jargon terms and laws there are in the *Harry Potter* universe. They have their own established governments, career paths, school paths, and internal history, right on top of the history of our own world. For this, you're going to need to employ some of the exercises and thought processes we've gone over up to this point. But there's going to be a bit more involved stuff here. So below I've listed some questions you should consider asking yourself while working:

- Is there a government or system of order for this world? Is it anarchy? What do they call their leaders?

- Is there a caste system or career hierarchy? Is it capitalist or more functional forms of labor?

- What is the nature of the divide between this world and the "real" one? Is it a secret? Are their rules about interacting with people? Is it a peaceful existence? Has there been war in the past?

To help you practice, you can apply these questions to a known work of low fantasy like *Harry Potter* and *His Dark Materials* to get a sense for how you can model your own answers. Once you've got a grounding with some basics, you can move forward with the rest of it. The key to this is building as much of the foundation of the world as you can and then letting the people within the world and the functions of it come to life on their own.

But then there's high fantasy. This is the type of world building that is the most involved and most difficult. You're going to be putting to use everything you've used up until this point plus some extra stuff. This is another step that you're going to find a lot of internet help for out there. There's plenty of world building worksheets, not unlike characters, that exist and many of them are helpful. But the thing is…where do you start? Where does one start when it comes to building an entire universe?

- Step 1: Decide where it takes place. By this I mean decide if this world exists as some form of Earth (like Middle-earth), a parallel universe (like *His Dark Materials*), or an entirely different planet (like *Skyrim*). Placing this place physically is an easy step to get through and a good place to start. It can also inherently answer some other questions for you (like the scientific laws of this world, for example).

- Step 2: Decide the time. This means decide the analogous timeline in which this takes place (is it medieval technology, steampunk, futuristic?) All fantasy worlds have a basis in our real world so you can base your technology, architecture, and clothing styles on whatever time period you choose. This another step that can help get you ahead in answering other questions by making this choice.

- Step 3: Pick a government style. This is more important and more nuanced than it might seem. The government you choose and follow can be very indicative of a lot of other things in the world. For example, consider America: a republic with influences of democracy this freedom has led to a reliance on capitalism which in turn created an individualistic culture of ambition and self-progress. The governments we choose for ourselves can lead to several other choices about the society. So you might want to do research here to come up with a government system that works for you and historically has caused different fluctuations in the rest of the culture and society of your world.

- Step 4: Develop a history. You don't need a detailed history, in fact, you can just make a timeline and write down three events that helped shape this world. If we were to pick some from our own we would say the Renaissance, the discovery of America, and the World Wars. Obviously, dozens more happened, but right now just pick three. Tell yourself why they're important. From them, you'll likely get other events that spiral off in a domino effect.

- Step 5: Mapping. This actually goes along with history more than anything else. If you look at a map of Westeros or the maps in Skyrim, and you'll see dozens of castles, and ruins, and natural features with names that hint at a real, lived in history. This will help not only with story mapping if you need locations, but build the world, the technology, the history, and just how long it's existed for.

- Step 6: Does magic exist? Even if the answer is no, this question isn't as simple as it seems. There are many questions that can branch off of this one. For example, you can ask yourself if the lack of magic is important? Is it illegal? Was there magic once? Is it just a story people tell? In *A Song of Ice and Fire*, magic is something of a bedtime story until the dragons return and magic subsequently returns to the world as well. In the BBC series *Merlin*, magic is outlawed in Camelot. This is a question that goes for a lot of parts of your world. The absence of something doesn't mean it isn't relevant to the story or the setting. Is there a reason it's not there?

- Step 7: How do your characters feel about everything? Review everything you've answered and mapped out until now and decide how your characters feel about the state of things. No one is neutral, look at yourself after all. Do you ever have absolutely no opinion on an election or a historical event? Your characters are going to be the same. This is where world building and character building is going to overlap quite a bit.

Does it all seem scary and overwhelming? It doesn't have to. This is actually one of the most fun parts of the process. This is where you get to have fun without the anxiety of hitting word counts or making your prose as perfect as possible. You can erase and rewrite this part as much as you want. You can change it in the middle of working on a story If you really need to. This world you create is flexible. You can listen to it and see what's working and what isn't.

But these steps and outline guides will help you to make that malleable base. You can go from there to create whatever world you need to.

CHAPTER 5: DRAFTS AND SECOND DRAFTS

I know you probably hear from varying people that different parts of writing are all the hardest part of writing. The entire process is difficult, but working on drafts and editing can be mentally taxing. It can be physically taxing as well. People don't seem to realize all that mentally and physically goes into crafting a story. You getting exhausted is not only common but a sign that you're doing things right.

Drafting is a long and arduous process and it might even be a painful process because you could be completely enamored with one of your sections but it, unfortunately, needs to go. These things happen but you can always return to your outlines from before to figure things out. Below are some things to keep in mind while editing and drafting your work…

Can You Say It Quicker?

Subtlety and minimalistic wording are incredibly important. If you're someone who went to a college program in writing you'll likely remember several semesters of being told to "write like Hemingway", saying things as quickly and swiftly as possible. Well, there's something to that, whether you agreed or not. You don't need to cut things down to the bare-bones that Hemingway did, especially if that's not what your voice is about when it comes to writing.

But. There's no escaping the red pen and hitting the paragraphs with it. You want to edit sentences as if you're getting paid a dollar for every word you remove. This is a very micro level of editing, done sentence to sentence but it works and it's important to so don't skip on it. Not to mention the method can be applied to larger parts of the story as well. Everything in straightforwardness. That being said, of course, if you're writing high fantasy then several layers of exposition and wordiness are part of the genre, still there's trimming that can be accomplished there as well, don't skip it.

There's a famous saying "kill your darlings" referring to killing off your favorite characters if you need to for the sake of the story. But that also applies to things like this: sections you love but need to go to get the story moving in the needed flow.

Talking Too Much?

This is one of the biggest struggles writers face in situations of dialogue. Just like any of us, characters like to hear themselves talk. Sometimes they will not shut up, there are situations where they talk and talk and talk and you're not sure how to make them stop. You might have an entire page of nothing but back and forth dialogue. You'll want to chop that down. While it's better to get something said in dialogue than to preach it to the reader, you also don't want them reading entire pages of dialogue, this is a book, not a play.

Sometimes a lot of dialogue is good, it's important to get the information out. But there is a difference between writing a scene of well-constructed dialogue and letting the scene get away from you completely. If there are lines you absolutely don't want to cut out during the editing process you can always add in more prose to break the dialogue up, make it visually easier on the reader. But the best way to deal with this is to avoid it all together and make your dialogue scenes short and sweet.

Use Your Outlines

The outlines you created before you started writing aren't just for writing itself, you can use them constantly throughout the process to go back and figure out what you need to fix and where. They're your Bible and guiding framework. They helped you overcome writer's block and now they will help you deal with making sure the story you've created matches the one you've intended.

Now, this doesn't mean if a scene doesn't completely fit the version of it that was outlined that you need to cut it. But use the outline to bargain with yourself about the situation. Use the outline to figure out what exactly works and how you can best resolve a situation of confusion for yourself. The outline won't be perfect, but it's always a place to come back to you if you need to rework something.

Don't Let Drafts Scare You

There are some writers who are perfectly content with writing an entire book several times. By this, I mean completely rewriting it. We're lucky today that we have word processing software that can alter any portion of text at any time without worrying about hitting the backspace button. But this is a new invention for writers. Before this, editing and drafting meant writing things a second time. It was a lot more work than we can imagine now. Harper Lee had at least 5 drafts of *To Kill a Mockingbird*, 5 full versions of the story.

Today, we don't really need to rewrite something if it bothers us or needs improvement. We simply patch it up within a word document and move on. So don't be afraid to do that and label the different versions of this story as your drafts. It helps to save various versions of the story to compare sections and dialogue between drafts. Sometimes change isn't always better. Sometimes it helps to have a discourse between your versions of a story. So don't be afraid to go back, no change is permanent and not every change is the right one.

Get a Workshop

I remember once a professor telling us in college to stop complaining about constantly workshopping because it was a resource we would not have outside of college without some serious work. And she was right. Getting friends to read and edit your work is a lot harder when you're not being forced to do it for a grade.

But this is something you can't skip. You need to get outside feedback but you're too close to your work to ever look at it without a bias. So do everything you can to get someone to read your work and give you feedback as a reader. If there is a glaring issue, it needs to be handled here, before an agent or publisher has the chance to make it a reason to pass on your work.

Do some research, you can find that a writing workshop might already exist at the local library or bookstore. If there isn't one, don't be afraid of starting one. If you went to school for writing, then you've got your built-in network of writers you can go to for help.

Editing and drafting can be a grueling process, but it's going to get you one step closer to seeing your book in the flesh, so take care during it and give it your all.

CHAPTER 6: SELLING YOUR WORK

This is the part that they don't often teach in school. I can't recall ever having a class about how to sell and publish your book. There was only one moment I recall where a workshop professor told us that a collection of short stories was nice, but publishers would ask for your novel first. That was the only time during my college years that anyone hinted at the business side of this.

So, how does that business side word? The first thing is to realize, however, unfortunately, this is a business. This is a marketplace that people are using to sell products. Writing has become a form of goods production. It takes away from the art form, it might be a little bit heartbreaking, but it's the way things are now. So you need to realize that quickly and move forward from it. It's going to be an unfortunate truth that haunts you. I've had agents tell me they absolutely loved the work, the characters, everything, had no complaints, but just didn't know how to market the work.

The fact is, the agent's opinion, even the slush pile readers at publishing houses, it's all just one person's opinion. And because you're going person to person, virtually knocking on doors, it can feel like finding a needle in a haystack. The problem is that the publishing world moves at a glacial pace, taking weeks between replies and full years to put something into print.

Option 1: Finding an Agent

The most popular option for authors is to find an agent to

represent your work after you've finished it and polished it and decided you're happy with where it stands now. To do this you'll first want to find agents who are actually accepting submissions. They can get mighty cranky if you even think of bugging them with your plebian requests if they didn't ask for it. So a good place to start is Writer's Digest. They keep a list of agents who have updated their submissions and put out new requests for submissions. A more comprehensive resource is QueryTracker which gives you a plethora of metadata about agents and you can see their response times for other writers. You can also check social media to see if agents have posted about their query situation.

Either way, finding an agent starts with a query letter. The components to this are introduction and pitch of work with lots of genre buzzwords, word count, a list of works that this is similar to, a short personal biography, and any samples below that that have been requested. What you'll want to do is create a query form letter and then change the details of it as it pertains to different agents you're messaging. This saves you time and, if you get responses, you'll want to reuse that query form as much as possible since it's clearly working.

- Step 1: They response asking for a partial. There are two ways an agent can respond to an initial query: request for full or request for partial. A partial is more common, especially for bigger agents since they can usually figure out in the first couple of chapters if they plan on pursuing this work. Unusually a partial is the first 50 pages. If they ask for this it may come with a request for a synopsis as well so they can see how the story will end.

- Step 2: They liked the partial and now want a full. At this stage, they'll ask for the rest of the manuscript. This is why it's important to never query an agent with a work in progress manuscript. There's always a chance they could ask for the whole thing within minutes of your email (I've had it happen) and you could blow your chance and the professional relationship with this agent if you don't have something prepared for them.

- Step 3: Offer of representation. After a talk and after you inform any other agents who have samples of your work and are still deciding, you take up the agent on their offer of representation. You're not done writing. The agency will have edits for you, small things usually. And this won't be the last time someone sends you edits.

- Step 4: Finding a publisher. This part can be as long and frustrating as finding an agent but the agent does take on the burden of the work so you get some stress relief...some. Don't get discouraged, Mark Z. Danielewski's bestseller *House of Leaves* was rejected by 32 publishers. Again, it's a needle in a haystack and finding just one person who believes in the story. It might take a while, but don't let it discourage you.

- Step 5: It works. Now do it again. After arduous legal documents, you've got your deal, you've decided on an advance, the royalty rate, and everything else. You're set to do your edits; the book is headed for publication. Congrats, you're going to have to do this all again for your next book.

Option 2: Straight to Publishers

This is basically only an option for indie publishers. Almost none of the Big Five or their imprints are willing to read work from authors who don't come agented. They do this to weed down their submission pile because, otherwise, it would be impossible to tackle. But many independent publishing houses not only accept submissions from unrepresented authors but encourage it. Agents, after all, are a new invention. Writers have existed for hundreds of years without agents. So if you're willing to be published on a smaller scale, then this is a great option for you.

It involves the same ingredients as querying an agent and they'll still likely ask for a partial and then a full. But the nice thing about it is that, when it's done, you're going right to publishing instead of having to go through the selling it step all over again.

Indie publishing has become a thriving community, with annual awards for independently published works and plenty of indie works have made it onto the bestseller list without the backing of a massive and overblown publishing house. It's possible to do it this way if you find trying to play the market game just isn't working for you.

Option 3: Self-Publishing

For many authors, this is the last resort because of the stigma surrounding it. But, for certain genres and works, this is the best option. Createspace is the most common self-publishing resource but Pronoun is another good one. You can do this entirely on your own, control the entire process. The only downside is your fronting the bill yourself (usually anywhere between $1,000-$5,000) and you have to do all the marketing yourself. So this isn't recommended for first-time authors. You'll want to build up a base first, a place where you can plant the seeds of your book. But once you've got that, there's nothing stopping your book from being a hit. And you get to keep the profits yourself, no agent who gets a percentage or publisher who offers you royalties.

Don't discount this option because of pride or ego. Even if it's not how you imagine selling and publishing your book, at the end of if you'll have a published work and that's far better than nothing.

Option 4: The Internet

This might fall under self-publishing but it's not exactly as straightforward. There are some works out there that started out on the Internet. Think of it like a newer version of putting out chapters in monthly newspapers like Sherlock Holmes used to be published. For this, however, you're putting out pieces of the story on blogs, YouTube videos, or other outlets. *Penpal* by Dathan Auerbach started out as posts on a Reddit board before it went to publication and became a huge hit. It's one way to get yourself a following before you actually get out there and publish something. It doesn't guarantee anything, but it isn't a bad way to start things out for yourself. It also works as a great way to get some early feedback from your work.

Option 5: Competitions and Magazines

If you have parts of the story that can stand on their own,

consider sending them in as short stories to various competitions. Some competitions have monetary prizes and even include publication rights as one of them. And if not, it's great to get your work out there and you can offer any placement you get in the competition into your bio in your query letters to agents and publishers.

The only downside here is you'll need to read the fine print because some publications want exclusive publishing rights to work you submit but there are so many competitions and magazines out there that you have your pick of the lot for the ones that won't try to make things too hard on you. So do some research and see if anything works for you in the realm of short story competitions.

Ultimately, selling your work is very objective. It doesn't seem to match very well. Writing is a subjective and artful experience while trying to get it sold depends on some very objective market facts. It's not fair and it might make things tough for you, especially at the beginning. But all you need is one good book and one strong believer in your work and then what can happen is limitless.

CONCLUSION

Writing a book is not easy, despite how many people try to do it, not many of them know how to do it well. But if you've got passion and drive and a love for what you're doing, then you're going to go far. The biggest piece of advice I can give you at the end of this is to not let your head go down and to always keep trying. One failure does not sum up a career and one person's opinion is not truth.

This is tough because this is you putting yourself and your work out there. But if you have the courage and drive to do it, it can turn out amazing for you. So use this book as a guide to get yourself writing and get cracking on your work. It's going to take a lot of discipline and a lot of self-motivation but, if you've already committed to the idea of writing, then you're already halfway there.

By reading this book, you've already taken an important first step towards getting your work published and seeing through to your goals. Research and preparation are key. So take note of the advice here and do research of your own. There's no one right way to write a book and there truly is no wrong way. You can do things however you need to get your goals accomplished. So good luck and get writing!

LIKE THIS BOOK?

Check us out online or follow us on social media for exclusive deals and news on new releases!

 https://www.pinnaclepublish.com

 https://www.facebook.com/PinnaclePublishers/

 https://twitter.com/PinnaclePub

 https://www.instagram.com/pinnaclepublishers/

Made in the USA
San Bernardino, CA
10 January 2018